50 Around the World Dishes

By: Kelly Johnson

Table of Contents

- Pad Thai (Thailand)
- Coq au Vin (France)
- Paella (Spain)
- Tandoori Chicken (India)
- Moussaka (Greece)
- Bulgogi (Korea)
- Jollof Rice (Nigeria)
- Ceviche (Peru)
- Peking Duck (China)
- Wiener Schnitzel (Austria)
- Goulash (Hungary)
- Biryani (India)
- Pho (Vietnam)
- Feijoada (Brazil)
- Shepherd's Pie (UK)
- Borscht (Russia/Ukraine)
- Chiles en Nogada (Mexico)

- Bobotie (South Africa)
- Chicken Adobo (Philippines)
- Shakshuka (Israel)
- Hainanese Chicken Rice (Singapore)
- Rendang (Indonesia)
- Pierogi (Poland)
- Beef Stroganoff (Russia)
- Tom Yum Soup (Thailand)
- Tagine (Morocco)
- Lasagna (Italy)
- Kimchi Jjigae (Korea)
- Fish and Chips (UK)
- Khachapuri (Georgia)
- Arepas (Venezuela)
- Tabbouleh (Lebanon)
- Okonomiyaki (Japan)
- Koshari (Egypt)
- Laksa (Malaysia)
- Churrasco (Argentina)

- Cassoulet (France)
- Banitsa (Bulgaria)
- Currywurst (Germany)
- Tamales (Mexico)
- Satay (Indonesia)
- Rogan Josh (India)
- Empanadas (Argentina)
- Nasi Goreng (Indonesia)
- Souvlaki (Greece)
- Fufu with Egusi Soup (Nigeria)
- Chicken Kiev (Ukraine)
- Sushi (Japan)
- Smørrebrød (Denmark)
- Lomo Saltado (Peru)

Pad Thai (Thailand)

Ingredients:

- 8 oz rice noodles
- 2 tbsp vegetable oil
- 2 cloves garlic, minced
- 2 eggs, lightly beaten
- 1 cup cooked shrimp or chicken
- 1 cup bean sprouts
- 2 green onions, sliced
- 1/4 cup crushed peanuts
- 2 tbsp fish sauce
- 1 tbsp soy sauce
- 1 tbsp tamarind paste
- 1 tbsp brown sugar
- Lime wedges and fresh cilantro for garnish

Instructions:

1. Soak rice noodles in warm water for 20–30 minutes, then drain.
2. In a wok or skillet, heat oil over medium heat. Sauté garlic until fragrant.
3. Push garlic to one side, pour in eggs, and scramble until just set.

4. Add noodles, cooked shrimp or chicken, fish sauce, soy sauce, tamarind paste, and brown sugar. Toss well to coat.

5. Stir in bean sprouts and green onions. Cook for another 2–3 minutes.

6. Serve with crushed peanuts, lime wedges, and cilantro.

Coq au Vin (France)

Ingredients:

- 4 chicken thighs and 4 drumsticks
- Salt and pepper
- 2 tbsp olive oil
- 4 oz pancetta or bacon, diced
- 1 onion, chopped
- 2 carrots, chopped
- 2 cloves garlic, minced
- 2 tbsp flour
- 2 cups red wine
- 1 cup chicken broth
- 1 bay leaf, 2 sprigs thyme
- 8 oz mushrooms, halved

Instructions:

1. Season chicken with salt and pepper. Brown in oil and set aside.
2. In the same pot, cook pancetta, onion, carrots, and garlic until softened.
3. Sprinkle in flour, stir for 1–2 minutes. Add wine and broth, then herbs.
4. Return chicken to the pot. Cover and simmer 45–60 minutes.

5. Add mushrooms and cook uncovered for 15 more minutes.

6. Serve with mashed potatoes or crusty bread.

Paella (Spain)

Ingredients:

- 2 tbsp olive oil
- 1 onion, chopped
- 1 bell pepper, chopped
- 2 cloves garlic, minced
- 1 1/2 cups Arborio or bomba rice
- 1/2 tsp saffron threads
- 1 tsp smoked paprika
- 3 cups chicken or seafood broth
- 1 cup diced tomatoes
- 1/2 lb shrimp
- 1/2 lb mussels or clams
- 1/2 lb chicken or chorizo
- Lemon wedges and parsley for garnish

Instructions:

1. Heat oil in a wide skillet. Cook onion, pepper, and garlic until soft.
2. Stir in rice, saffron, paprika, and broth. Bring to a simmer.
3. Add tomatoes and chicken/chorizo. Simmer uncovered for 10 minutes.

4. Add shrimp and shellfish. Cover and cook 10–15 minutes more.

5. Remove from heat, let rest 5 minutes. Garnish with lemon and parsley.

Tandoori Chicken (India)

Ingredients:

- 4 chicken thighs or drumsticks
- 1 cup plain yogurt
- 2 tbsp lemon juice
- 1 tbsp garam masala
- 2 tsp paprika
- 1 tsp turmeric
- 1 tsp cumin
- 1 tsp chili powder
- 1 tbsp minced garlic
- 1 tbsp grated ginger
- Salt to taste

Instructions:

1. Mix all spices, yogurt, lemon juice, garlic, and ginger in a bowl.
2. Score chicken, then coat in marinade. Refrigerate 4+ hours or overnight.
3. Preheat oven to 425°F (220°C) or use a grill. Bake or grill chicken 25–30 minutes until charred and cooked through.
4. Serve with naan, rice, and yogurt sauce.

Moussaka (Greece)

Ingredients:

- 2 eggplants, sliced
- 2 tbsp olive oil
- 1 lb ground lamb or beef
- 1 onion, chopped
- 2 cloves garlic, minced
- 1 can crushed tomatoes
- 1/2 tsp cinnamon
- Salt and pepper
- 2 tbsp flour
- 2 tbsp butter
- 2 cups milk
- 1/2 cup grated Parmesan
- 1 egg, beaten

Instructions:

1. Salt eggplant slices, let sit 30 minutes, then rinse and pat dry.
2. Sauté eggplant in olive oil until golden. Set aside.
3. Brown meat with onion and garlic. Add tomatoes, cinnamon, salt, and pepper. Simmer 20 minutes.

4. Make béchamel: melt butter, whisk in flour, then milk. Cook until thick. Add Parmesan and egg.

5. Layer eggplant, meat sauce, and béchamel in a baking dish.

6. Bake at 375°F (190°C) for 40 minutes until golden.

Bulgogi (Korea)

Ingredients:

- 1 lb beef sirloin, thinly sliced
- 1/4 cup soy sauce
- 2 tbsp brown sugar
- 1 tbsp sesame oil
- 2 cloves garlic, minced
- 1 tsp grated ginger
- 1/2 onion, sliced
- 2 green onions, chopped
- 1 tsp sesame seeds

Instructions:

1. Mix soy sauce, sugar, sesame oil, garlic, ginger, and onions in a bowl.
2. Marinate beef in the mixture for at least 1 hour.
3. Grill or pan-fry beef over high heat until cooked and caramelized.
4. Garnish with sesame seeds and serve with rice and kimchi.

Jollof Rice (Nigeria)

Ingredients:

- 2 cups long-grain rice
- 1/4 cup vegetable oil
- 1 onion, chopped
- 1 red bell pepper, chopped
- 2 tomatoes, chopped
- 2 tbsp tomato paste
- 1 tsp paprika
- 1 tsp thyme
- 1 tsp curry powder
- 3 cups chicken broth
- Salt and pepper to taste

Instructions:

1. Blend peppers, tomatoes, and half the onion into a smooth paste.
2. Heat oil and sauté remaining onion. Add tomato paste and cook 2 minutes.
3. Stir in blended mix, spices, and cook 10–15 minutes.
4. Add rice and broth. Cover and simmer on low 20–30 minutes until rice is tender.
5. Fluff with a fork and serve hot.

Ceviche (Peru)

Ingredients:

- 1 lb fresh firm white fish (like sea bass), diced
- 1/2 red onion, thinly sliced
- 1–2 limes, juiced
- 1 lemon, juiced
- 1 small chili pepper, minced
- 1 tbsp chopped cilantro
- Salt to taste
- Corn and sweet potato (optional, for serving)

Instructions:

1. Combine fish, citrus juice, chili, and onion in a bowl.
2. Cover and refrigerate for 20–30 minutes, until fish turns opaque.
3. Stir in cilantro and salt.
4. Serve chilled with boiled corn and sweet potato slices.

Peking Duck (China)

Ingredients:

- 1 whole duck (4–5 lbs)
- 2 tbsp honey
- 2 tbsp soy sauce
- 1 tbsp rice vinegar
- 1 tsp five-spice powder
- Pancakes, hoisin sauce, cucumber, and scallions for serving

Instructions:

1. Rinse and pat the duck dry. Prick the skin all over with a skewer.
2. Mix honey, soy sauce, vinegar, and five-spice. Brush onto the duck.
3. Air-dry the duck uncovered in the fridge overnight for crispy skin.
4. Roast at 375°F (190°C) for 1.5–2 hours, turning occasionally.
5. Serve with pancakes, hoisin, cucumber, and scallions.

Wiener Schnitzel (Austria)

Ingredients:

- 4 veal cutlets (or chicken/pork)
- Salt and pepper
- 1/2 cup flour
- 2 eggs, beaten
- 1 cup breadcrumbs
- Oil for frying
- Lemon wedges for serving

Instructions:

1. Pound cutlets thin, season with salt and pepper.
2. Dredge in flour, dip in egg, then coat with breadcrumbs.
3. Heat oil in a skillet. Fry cutlets 2–3 minutes per side until golden.
4. Drain on paper towels and serve with lemon wedges.

Goulash (Hungary)

Ingredients:

- 2 tbsp lard or vegetable oil
- 2 onions, finely chopped
- 2 lbs beef chuck, cut into cubes
- 2 tbsp Hungarian paprika
- 2 cloves garlic, minced
- 1 bell pepper, chopped
- 2 tomatoes, chopped
- 3 cups beef broth
- 2 potatoes, diced (optional)
- Salt and pepper to taste

Instructions:

1. Heat oil in a large pot, sauté onions until golden.
2. Add beef, brown on all sides. Stir in paprika and garlic.
3. Add bell pepper, tomatoes, and broth. Bring to a boil.
4. Simmer covered for 1.5–2 hours, until beef is tender.
5. Add potatoes in the last 30 minutes if using.
6. Serve hot with crusty bread or egg noodles.

Biryani (India)

Ingredients:

- 2 cups basmati rice, soaked
- 1 lb chicken or lamb, cubed
- 1 cup yogurt
- 1 large onion, sliced
- 2 cloves garlic, minced
- 1 tbsp ginger, grated
- 2 tsp garam masala
- 1 tsp turmeric
- 1/2 tsp chili powder
- 1/2 tsp saffron soaked in 2 tbsp warm milk
- Fresh mint and cilantro for garnish
- 3 cups water or broth

Instructions:

1. Marinate meat with yogurt, garlic, ginger, and spices for 1+ hour.
2. Fry onion until crispy and golden, set aside.
3. Cook meat in a pot until partially done.
4. Layer half-cooked rice over the meat. Drizzle with saffron milk and fried onions.

5. Cover tightly and steam on low heat for 20–30 minutes.

6. Fluff before serving. Garnish with mint and cilantro.

Pho (Vietnam)

Ingredients:

- 1 lb beef bones or brisket
- 1 onion and 1 piece ginger, charred
- 2 star anise, 1 cinnamon stick
- 1 tbsp coriander seeds
- 1 tbsp fish sauce
- 6 cups water
- 8 oz rice noodles
- Thin slices of raw beef (sirloin or eye of round)
- Garnishes: bean sprouts, lime wedges, Thai basil, chili, hoisin, sriracha

Instructions:

1. Simmer bones, onion, ginger, spices, and fish sauce in water for 2–3 hours. Strain.
2. Soak and cook rice noodles according to package.
3. Place noodles and raw beef in bowls.
4. Pour hot broth over top to cook the beef.
5. Add desired garnishes and serve.

Feijoada (Brazil)

Ingredients:

- 1 lb black beans, soaked
- 1/2 lb pork shoulder, cubed
- 1/2 lb smoked sausage, sliced
- 1/2 lb bacon or salted pork
- 1 onion, chopped
- 3 cloves garlic, minced
- 2 bay leaves
- Salt and pepper to taste
- Orange slices and rice for serving

Instructions:

1. Brown bacon and pork in a large pot. Add onion and garlic, sauté.
2. Add beans, sausage, bay leaves, and enough water to cover.
3. Simmer 2–3 hours until beans are soft and meat is tender.
4. Season to taste. Serve with rice and orange slices.

Shepherd's Pie (UK)

Ingredients:

- 1 lb ground lamb or beef
- 1 onion, chopped
- 2 carrots, chopped
- 2 cloves garlic, minced
- 1 tbsp tomato paste
- 1 tbsp Worcestershire sauce
- 1 cup beef broth
- 2 cups mashed potatoes
- Salt and pepper to taste
- 1/2 cup grated cheese (optional)

Instructions:

1. Brown meat with onion, garlic, and carrots.
2. Stir in tomato paste, Worcestershire, broth. Simmer until thickened.
3. Transfer to baking dish, top with mashed potatoes and cheese.
4. Bake at 375°F (190°C) for 25–30 minutes until golden.

Borscht (Russia/Ukraine)

Ingredients:

- 3 medium beets, peeled and grated
- 1 onion, chopped
- 1 carrot, chopped
- 1 potato, diced
- 1/2 small cabbage, shredded
- 4 cups beef or vegetable broth
- 2 tbsp tomato paste
- 1 bay leaf
- Salt, pepper, and vinegar to taste
- Sour cream and dill for serving

Instructions:

1. Sauté onion and carrot in oil until soft.
2. Add beets and tomato paste, cook 5 minutes.
3. Add broth, potatoes, cabbage, and bay leaf. Simmer until vegetables are tender.
4. Season with salt, pepper, and a splash of vinegar.
5. Serve hot with sour cream and dill.

Chiles en Nogada (Mexico)

Ingredients:

- 6 poblano peppers, roasted and peeled
- 1 lb ground pork or beef
- 1/2 onion, chopped
- 2 cloves garlic, minced
- 1 apple and 1 pear, diced
- 1/2 cup dried fruit (raisins, etc.)
- 1/2 tsp cinnamon
- Salt and pepper

Nogada Sauce:

- 1 cup walnuts, soaked and peeled
- 1/2 cup milk
- 4 oz cream cheese
- 1 tbsp sugar
- Salt to taste

Toppings:

- Pomegranate seeds
- Fresh parsley

Instructions:

1. Sauté onion, garlic, meat, then add fruit and spices. Cook until tender.

2. Blend sauce ingredients until smooth.

3. Stuff peppers with meat filling.

4. Pour walnut sauce over top. Garnish with pomegranate seeds and parsley.

Bobotie (South Africa)

Ingredients:

- 1 lb ground beef or lamb
- 1 onion, chopped
- 1 slice bread soaked in milk
- 2 tbsp curry powder
- 2 tbsp chutney or apricot jam
- 1 tbsp vinegar
- 1/2 tsp turmeric
- 1/4 cup raisins
- 2 eggs
- 1/2 cup milk

Instructions:

1. Sauté onion, add meat and cook until browned.
2. Squeeze milk from bread and crumble it into meat. Add spices, chutney, raisins.
3. Transfer to baking dish.
4. Beat eggs with milk and pour over top.
5. Bake at 350°F (175°C) for 35–40 minutes until golden and set.

Chicken Adobo (Philippines)

Ingredients:

- 2 lbs chicken thighs or drumsticks
- 1/2 cup soy sauce
- 1/3 cup vinegar
- 5 cloves garlic, smashed
- 2 bay leaves
- 1 tsp black peppercorns
- 1 tbsp brown sugar (optional)
- 1 cup water

Instructions:

1. Combine all ingredients in a pot. Marinate 30 minutes.
2. Bring to a boil, then simmer uncovered for 30–40 minutes.
3. Reduce sauce until slightly thickened.
4. Serve over rice.

Shakshuka (Israel)

Ingredients:

- 1 tbsp olive oil
- 1 onion, chopped
- 1 bell pepper, chopped
- 2 cloves garlic, minced
- 1 tsp cumin
- 1/2 tsp paprika
- 1/4 tsp chili flakes
- 1 can diced tomatoes
- 4–6 eggs
- Salt and pepper
- Fresh cilantro or parsley

Instructions:

1. Sauté onion and pepper in oil until soft. Add garlic and spices.
2. Stir in tomatoes, simmer 10 minutes.
3. Make small wells and crack eggs in.
4. Cover and cook until eggs are set.
5. Garnish with herbs. Serve with bread.

Hainanese Chicken Rice (Singapore)

Ingredients:

- 1 whole chicken
- 1 tbsp salt
- 5 slices ginger
- 5 cloves garlic
- 4 cups chicken stock
- 2 cups jasmine rice
- 2 tbsp chicken fat or oil
- Salt, to taste

For Sauce:

- 3 tbsp soy sauce
- 1 tbsp sesame oil
- Chili-garlic sauce (optional)

Instructions:

1. Rub chicken with salt and rinse. Boil with ginger and garlic until cooked (45 mins).
2. Remove, set aside, and submerge in ice water for tender skin.
3. Sauté garlic in chicken fat, add rice and toast for 2–3 mins.

4. Add 4 cups chicken stock and cook rice.

5. Serve chicken sliced over rice with sauce and broth on the side.

Rendang (Indonesia)

Ingredients:

- 2 lbs beef chuck, cubed
- 1 can coconut milk
- 4 cloves garlic
- 1 inch ginger
- 4 shallots
- 1 stalk lemongrass
- 1 tsp turmeric
- 2 kaffir lime leaves
- 1 tbsp chili paste
- Salt and sugar to taste

Instructions:

1. Blend garlic, shallots, ginger, and spices into a paste.
2. Sauté paste until fragrant, then add beef and stir.
3. Pour in coconut milk, lemongrass, and lime leaves.
4. Simmer uncovered for 2–3 hours, stirring occasionally, until sauce thickens and meat is tender.
5. Serve with steamed rice.

Pierogi (Poland)

Ingredients (Dough):

- 2 cups flour
- 1/2 tsp salt
- 1 egg
- 1/2 cup sour cream
- 1/4 cup butter

Filling Options:

- Mashed potato and cheese
- Sauerkraut and mushrooms
- Ground meat

Instructions:

1. Mix dough ingredients and knead until smooth. Rest for 30 mins.
2. Roll dough thin, cut circles, and place filling in center.
3. Fold and seal edges. Boil until they float, about 3–4 minutes.
4. Optional: pan-fry with butter and onions before serving.

Beef Stroganoff (Russia)

Ingredients:

- 1 lb beef sirloin, thinly sliced
- 1 onion, sliced
- 1 cup mushrooms, sliced
- 2 tbsp flour
- 1 cup beef broth
- 1/2 cup sour cream
- 1 tbsp Dijon mustard
- Salt and pepper

Instructions:

1. Sear beef in batches, set aside.
2. Sauté onion and mushrooms, add flour, then broth.
3. Stir in mustard and sour cream. Add beef back in.
4. Simmer until thickened. Serve over egg noodles or rice.

Tom Yum Soup (Thailand)

Ingredients:

- 4 cups chicken broth
- 2 stalks lemongrass, smashed
- 4 kaffir lime leaves
- 2-inch galangal, sliced
- 1–2 Thai chilies, crushed
- 1 cup mushrooms
- 8–10 shrimp, peeled
- 2 tbsp fish sauce
- 1 tbsp lime juice
- Cilantro for garnish

Instructions:

1. Boil broth with lemongrass, lime leaves, and galangal.
2. Add chilies and mushrooms, cook 5 mins.
3. Add shrimp, cook until pink.
4. Stir in fish sauce and lime juice.
5. Garnish and serve hot.

Tagine (Morocco)

Ingredients:

- 2 lbs lamb or chicken
- 1 onion, chopped
- 2 cloves garlic, minced
- 1 tsp ground cumin
- 1 tsp ground cinnamon
- 1/2 tsp turmeric
- 1/2 cup dried apricots or raisins
- 1 can chickpeas
- 2 cups broth
- Fresh cilantro
- Olive oil, salt, pepper

Instructions:

1. Sear meat in olive oil, remove.
2. Sauté onion and garlic with spices.
3. Return meat, add dried fruit, chickpeas, and broth.
4. Cover and simmer for 1.5–2 hours.
5. Serve with couscous or bread.

Lasagna (Italy)

Ingredients:

- 9 lasagna noodles, cooked
- 1 lb ground beef
- 2 cups ricotta cheese
- 2 cups shredded mozzarella
- 1/2 cup Parmesan
- 1 egg
- 2 cups marinara sauce
- Basil and oregano

Instructions:

1. Brown beef, mix with marinara.
2. Mix ricotta, egg, and herbs.
3. In a baking dish, layer noodles, ricotta mix, meat sauce, and mozzarella.
4. Repeat layers and top with Parmesan.
5. Bake at 375°F (190°C) for 45 mins. Let cool 10 mins before serving.

Kimchi Jjigae (Korea)

Ingredients:

- 2 cups aged kimchi
- 1/2 onion, chopped
- 1/2 lb pork belly or tofu
- 1 tbsp gochugaru (Korean chili flakes)
- 1 tbsp soy sauce
- 1 tsp sesame oil
- 3 cups water or anchovy broth
- Green onions

Instructions:

1. In a pot, sauté pork with kimchi and onions.
2. Add gochugaru and soy sauce, stir well.
3. Pour in broth, simmer 20–30 mins.
4. Add tofu if using, cook 5 mins more.
5. Top with green onions, serve hot.

Fish and Chips (UK)

Ingredients:

- 4 cod or haddock fillets
- 1 cup flour
- 1 tsp baking powder
- 1 cup cold beer or soda water
- Salt and pepper
- 4 large potatoes, peeled and sliced
- Oil for frying

Instructions:

1. Heat oil for deep-frying.
2. Make batter: whisk flour, baking powder, salt, and beer until smooth.
3. Dredge fish in flour, then dip in batter.
4. Fry until golden, drain on paper towels.
5. Fry potatoes until crisp. Serve with tartar sauce and vinegar.

Khachapuri (Georgia)

Ingredients:

- 2 cups flour
- 1/2 tsp salt
- 1 tsp sugar
- 1/2 cup warm milk
- 1/2 tsp yeast
- 1 tbsp oil
- 1 cup feta and mozzarella cheese mix
- 1 egg

Instructions:

1. Mix yeast, sugar, and milk. Let sit 10 mins.
2. Add flour, salt, oil. Knead into dough. Rest 1 hour.
3. Roll into oval shape, form boat shape. Fill with cheese.
4. Bake at 450°F (230°C) for 12–15 mins. Crack egg on top and bake 5 more mins.
5. Mix yolk into hot cheese before eating.

Arepas (Venezuela)

Ingredients:

- 2 cups pre-cooked cornmeal (masarepa)
- 2.5 cups warm water
- 1 tsp salt
- Oil for frying

Filling Options:

- Shredded beef, cheese, black beans, avocado

Instructions:

1. Mix cornmeal, water, and salt. Let rest 5 mins.
2. Shape into 1-inch thick discs.
3. Cook on griddle 5–7 mins per side until golden.
4. Split open and fill with desired toppings.

Tabbouleh (Lebanon)

Ingredients:

- 1/2 cup fine bulgur wheat
- 4 firm tomatoes, finely diced
- 1 bunch parsley, finely chopped
- 1/2 bunch mint, finely chopped
- 4 green onions, thinly sliced
- 1/4 cup fresh lemon juice
- 1/4 cup olive oil
- Salt to taste

Instructions:

1. Soak bulgur in cold water for 20 minutes, then drain and squeeze dry.
2. In a bowl, mix bulgur, tomatoes, parsley, mint, and green onions.
3. Add lemon juice, olive oil, and salt.
4. Chill before serving. Great with romaine leaves or pita.

Okonomiyaki (Japan)

Ingredients:

- 1 cup flour
- 2/3 cup dashi or water
- 2 eggs
- 2 cups cabbage, finely shredded
- 4 strips bacon or pork belly
- Optional: green onion, tempura bits, pickled ginger

Toppings:

- Okonomiyaki sauce
- Japanese mayo
- Bonito flakes
- Nori flakes

Instructions:

1. Mix flour, dashi, eggs, and cabbage in a bowl.
2. Pour batter onto a greased skillet, shape into a circle.
3. Top with bacon, cook on medium heat for 5–7 minutes each side.
4. Drizzle with sauce and mayo, then top with bonito and nori.

Koshari (Egypt)

Ingredients:

- 1 cup rice
- 1 cup brown lentils
- 1 cup elbow macaroni
- 2 large onions, thinly sliced
- 3 cloves garlic, minced
- 1 can crushed tomatoes
- 1 tsp vinegar
- 1 tsp cumin
- Salt, pepper, oil

Instructions:

1. Cook lentils in salted water until tender.
2. Cook rice separately. Boil pasta and set aside.
3. Fry onions in oil until dark golden and crispy.
4. For sauce, sauté garlic, add tomatoes, vinegar, cumin, salt, and simmer.
5. To serve, layer rice, lentils, pasta, sauce, and crispy onions.

Laksa (Malaysia)

Ingredients:

- 1/2 lb shrimp or chicken
- 1 can coconut milk
- 2 cups chicken broth
- 2 tbsp laksa paste (or red curry paste)
- 1 tbsp fish sauce
- Rice noodles, cooked
- Toppings: bean sprouts, cilantro, boiled egg, lime wedges

Instructions:

1. Sauté laksa paste in oil until fragrant.
2. Add coconut milk and broth, bring to a simmer.
3. Add shrimp or chicken, cook until done.
4. Season with fish sauce.
5. Serve hot over noodles with toppings.

Churrasco (Argentina)

Ingredients:

- 2 lbs skirt or flank steak
- Salt and pepper
- Olive oil

Chimichurri Sauce:

- 1/2 cup parsley, finely chopped
- 2 cloves garlic, minced
- 2 tbsp oregano
- 1/4 cup red wine vinegar
- 1/2 cup olive oil
- Red pepper flakes, salt, pepper

Instructions:

1. Salt steak generously, let rest 30 minutes.
2. Grill over high heat 3–5 minutes per side.
3. For chimichurri, mix all ingredients in a bowl.
4. Slice steak thin and serve with chimichurri.

Cassoulet (France)

Ingredients:

- 1 lb white beans, soaked overnight
- 1/2 lb pork shoulder, cubed
- 4 sausages (Toulouse or similar)
- 1 duck leg confit (optional but traditional)
- 1 onion, chopped
- 2 cloves garlic
- 1 tbsp tomato paste
- 4 cups chicken stock
- Thyme, bay leaf, breadcrumbs

Instructions:

1. Sear meat and sausage. Set aside.
2. Sauté onion and garlic, stir in tomato paste.
3. Add beans, meats, herbs, and stock. Simmer 1.5 hours.
4. Transfer to baking dish, top with breadcrumbs, and bake at 350°F (175°C) for 45 mins–1 hour.

Banitsa (Bulgaria)

Ingredients:

- 1 package phyllo dough
- 1 cup crumbled feta
- 4 eggs
- 1 cup plain yogurt
- 1/4 cup butter, melted

Instructions:

1. Preheat oven to 375°F (190°C).
2. Mix eggs, feta, and yogurt in a bowl.
3. Layer 2 sheets of phyllo in greased pan, brush with butter, and add filling. Repeat layers.
4. Finish with butter on top.
5. Bake 35–40 minutes until golden. Serve warm.

Currywurst (Germany)

Ingredients:

- 4 bratwurst sausages
- 1 cup ketchup
- 1 tbsp curry powder
- 1 tsp Worcestershire sauce
- 1 tbsp vinegar
- 1 tsp sugar
- Oil

Instructions:

1. Grill or pan-fry sausages until browned.
2. In a saucepan, mix ketchup, curry powder, Worcestershire, vinegar, and sugar. Heat gently.
3. Slice sausages, pour sauce over, sprinkle with extra curry powder.
4. Serve with fries or bread rolls.

Tamales (Mexico)

Ingredients:

- 2 cups masa harina
- 1/2 cup lard or vegetable shortening
- 1 1/2 cups chicken broth
- 1 tsp baking powder
- Corn husks, soaked
- Filling: shredded chicken, pork, or beans with salsa

Instructions:

1. Beat lard until fluffy. Add masa, baking powder, and broth. Mix into soft dough.
2. Spread dough on corn husk, add filling, fold sides and bottom.
3. Steam upright for 1–1.5 hours until firm.
4. Let cool slightly before serving.

Satay (Indonesia)

Ingredients:

- 1 lb chicken or beef, thinly sliced
- Skewers, soaked in water

Marinade:

- 2 cloves garlic, minced
- 1 tbsp soy sauce
- 1 tbsp brown sugar
- 1 tsp turmeric
- 1 tsp coriander
- 1 tbsp oil

Peanut Sauce:

- 1/2 cup peanut butter
- 1 tbsp soy sauce
- 1 clove garlic
- 1 tsp chili sauce
- 1/2 cup water

Instructions:

1. Marinate meat for at least 1 hour.

2. Thread onto skewers, grill until charred and cooked through.

3. Blend sauce ingredients and heat gently until smooth.

4. Serve with warm peanut sauce and rice.

Rogan Josh (India)

Ingredients:

- 1 lb lamb, cubed
- 1 cup yogurt
- 1 large onion, finely sliced
- 3 garlic cloves, minced
- 1-inch ginger, grated
- 2 tsp paprika
- 1 tsp cayenne
- 1 tsp ground cumin
- 1 tsp ground coriander
- 1/2 tsp cinnamon
- 2-3 cardamom pods
- Salt, oil

Instructions:

1. Marinate lamb in yogurt, garlic, and spices for at least 1 hour.
2. Sauté onions in oil until golden. Add ginger, lamb with marinade, and cook until browned.
3. Add 1/2 cup water, cover, and simmer for 1–1.5 hours until tender.
4. Serve hot with basmati rice or naan.

Empanadas (Argentina)

Dough:

- 3 cups flour
- 1/2 cup butter
- 1 egg
- 1/2 cup water
- 1 tsp salt

Filling:

- 1/2 lb ground beef
- 1 onion, chopped
- 2 boiled eggs, chopped
- 1/4 cup green olives, chopped
- 1 tsp cumin
- 1 tsp paprika
- Salt and pepper

Instructions:

1. Make dough by combining all ingredients and kneading until smooth. Chill 30 minutes.
2. Sauté onion, add beef and spices. Once cooked, stir in eggs and olives.

3. Roll dough, cut circles, add filling, fold, seal, and crimp.

4. Bake at 400°F (200°C) for 20–25 minutes until golden.

Nasi Goreng (Indonesia)

Ingredients:

- 3 cups cooked rice (day-old preferred)
- 2 eggs
- 2 garlic cloves, minced
- 1 shallot, finely chopped
- 1 tbsp kecap manis (sweet soy sauce)
- 1 tbsp soy sauce
- 1 tsp chili paste (optional)
- Protein: shrimp, chicken, or tofu
- Oil

Instructions:

1. Scramble eggs in a wok, remove and set aside.
2. Sauté garlic, shallot, and protein until cooked.
3. Add rice, sauces, and chili paste. Stir-fry until well mixed.
4. Return eggs, stir through, and serve with a fried egg on top.

Souvlaki (Greece)

Ingredients:

- 1 lb pork or chicken, cubed
- Juice of 1 lemon
- 2 tbsp olive oil
- 2 garlic cloves, minced
- 1 tsp dried oregano
- Salt and pepper
- Skewers

Instructions:

1. Marinate meat in lemon juice, oil, garlic, oregano, salt, and pepper for at least 1 hour.
2. Thread onto skewers. Grill or broil for 10–12 minutes, turning occasionally.
3. Serve with pita, tzatziki, and salad.

Fufu with Egusi Soup (Nigeria)

Fufu:

- 2 cups cassava flour
- 3 cups water

Egusi Soup:

- 1/2 cup ground melon seeds (egusi)
- 1/2 lb meat or fish
- 2 cups spinach or bitterleaf
- 1/2 onion, chopped
- 1 cup palm oil
- 1 stock cube
- Salt, pepper, crayfish, and chili

Instructions:

1. Mix cassava flour with water, stir over medium heat until stretchy and smooth.
2. For soup, heat palm oil, sauté onion, add meat and spices. Simmer with water.
3. Stir in egusi paste, cook until thickened. Add greens and simmer.
4. Serve hot with fufu.

Chicken Kiev (Ukraine)

Ingredients:

- 2 chicken breasts
- 1/2 cup butter, mixed with parsley and garlic
- 1 egg, beaten
- Flour and breadcrumbs for coating
- Oil for frying

Instructions:

1. Flatten chicken breasts, place cold herbed butter in center, roll and seal tightly.
2. Chill, then coat in flour, egg, and breadcrumbs.
3. Fry until golden, then bake at 375°F (190°C) for 15–20 minutes.
4. Serve with mashed potatoes or greens.

Sushi (Japan)

Ingredients:

- 2 cups sushi rice
- 1/4 cup rice vinegar
- 1 tbsp sugar
- 1 tsp salt
- Nori sheets
- Fillings: raw fish, cucumber, avocado, crab, etc.

Instructions:

1. Rinse and cook rice. Mix vinegar, sugar, salt, and fold into rice.
2. On a bamboo mat, place nori shiny side down. Spread rice, leaving 1" border.
3. Add fillings, roll tightly, seal with water.
4. Slice with a wet knife and serve with soy sauce and wasabi.

Smørrebrød (Denmark)

Ingredients:

- Rye bread slices
- Butter
- Toppings: pickled herring, liver pâté, shrimp with mayo, boiled eggs, radish, roast beef

Instructions:

1. Butter each slice of rye bread generously.
2. Layer with toppings, arranging artfully.
3. Garnish with dill, capers, fried onions, or herbs.
4. Serve open-faced with a fork and knife.

Lomo Saltado (Peru)

Ingredients:

- 1 lb beef sirloin, sliced
- 1 red onion, sliced
- 1 tomato, sliced into wedges
- 1 tbsp soy sauce
- 1 tbsp vinegar
- 1 clove garlic
- Fries or potato wedges
- Cilantro for garnish

Instructions:

1. Sear beef in hot oil. Remove and set aside.
2. Sauté onion and garlic, then add tomato.
3. Return beef, add soy sauce and vinegar. Stir-fry quickly.
4. Toss with fries, garnish with cilantro, and serve with rice.